A Love Letter To God

Bayou Publishing

A Love Letter To God

by

Helen Smith Owen

A Love Letter to God
Copyright © 2025—Helen Smith Owen
ALL RIGHTS RESERVED UNDER U.S.,
PAN-AMERICAN, AND INTERNATIONAL
COPYRIGHT CONVENTIONS

All Scripture references are from the *Holy Bible, King James Version,* public domain.

Bayou Publishing, an imprint of McDougal & Associates, is dedicated to spreading the Gospel of the Lord Jesus Christ to as many people as possible in the shortest time possible.

Published by:

Bayou Publishing
www.ThePublishedWord.com

ISBN: 978-1-964665-38-2

Printed on demand in the U.S., the U.K. and Australia
For Worldwide Distribution

Dedication

I dedicate this book to all my spiritual mothers and fathers:

- Steve and Derene Schultz
- David Wilkerson
- Derek Prince
- Carolyn Sissom
- Karen Bovett
- Patsy Dupree
- John Hagee

To my large family down here on earth:

- Kelly Noel, my daughter
- Laura Elizabeth, my step-daughter
- My siblings:
  - Bert
  - Gary
  - Lizzie
  - Sharon
  - Stephen

- My grandchildren:
  - Jonathan
  - David
  - Daniel
  - Samuel
  - Kaia
  - And the new baby boy due February 13 of next year

I am forever grateful for the love and support of each one.

And to Jesus Christ, who, when I was still in sin and rebellion, cared enough for me to reveal Himself to me. He did this when I didn't even know that I was lost and in need of a Savior's love. What a miracle-working God!

Contents

Introduction 9

1. How Did I Get So Far from God? 11
2. Bad Choices Turned Around 24
3. Jesus Came into My Bedroom 31
4. Not My Will, but Thine Be Done 36
5. Being Sidelined for Years on End 38
6. On My Way to Heaven 44
7. My First Vision 49
8. What Do You Want to Get Out of the Bible? 54
9. The First True Miracle 58
10. Who Is Jesus? 67
11. Listening to the Holy Spirit 73
12. Learning to Forgive as Jesus Forgave 81
    Bible Portions that Have Blessed Me through the Years . 83
    Author Contact Page 85

And we know that all things work together for good to them that love God, to them who are the called according to his purpose.

– ROMANS 8:28

Introduction

What was I thinking? My life was out of control! For years, I had been living the quintessential party life and thought I was having the time of my life. In reality, I knew nothing of true life. Why was I surprised when everything started falling apart? So young, my second marriage was now failing, and I would soon find myself having to accept the total care and support of my precious daughter. What would happen to us now?

Life seemed to be a maze of unanswerable questions ... that is until I met Jesus. He changed everything. This is my story.

Helen Smith Owen
San Antonio, Texas

Chapter 1

How Did I Get So Far from God?

What happened to me that I got so far from God? I will tell you briefly what happened to me—sin, pure and simple. I had been listening to the wrong voices since high school, plus I had no proper church training. I was a good girl, but Jesus was not in my life. Very young I dated the wrong man and quickly married him, only to find that he was a raging alcoholic.

After nearly three years with this man, I finally got smart and got away from him. I was still in college at the time. My poor Mom and Daddy didn't know what to do. They were hurting for me, but they decided not to intervene. I was now an adult, they reasoned, and I would have to figure this out for myself. I surely didn't want to be married to an abuser, so I left the country and moved to Stockholm, Sweden for a year and finished up my last year of college at the University of Stockholm.

Why Stockholm? I knew someone there, an old friend from my high school days. His name was Magnus Mahl, and he had come to Texas as an exchange student years before. I had always had a crush on Magnus, so I jumped at this opportunity. Not knowing how to speak Swedish, I enrolled in the University of Stockholm's Institute for English Speaking Students and received my last few hours needed to graduate and had a ball doing it.

During that year, I not only traveled all over Sweden; I traveled all over Europe during vacations. It was glorious! Seriously, this was something I had always dreamed of doing, but little did I know the Lord had it all planned out for me ahead of time.

I met many wonderful people that year, people who were very loving and kind to me. I lived in the

Introduction

dorm with other Swedish students and learned to speak Swedish in two short months.

I also met a young Swedish pastor. He would attend our Friday parties and was the only one of us who had the good sense not to drink. That man sowed some important seeds into my life, and years later, after I had accepted Jesus as my Lord and Savior, the Lord, through His Holy Spirit, revealed to me that this precious man had prayed for me. It took seven years for his answer to come, but it did come, not in Sweden, but in Houston, Texas.

I had moved back to Houston where I taught school for many years. God was truly up to something. He knew I needed Him, even when I didn't. He waited patiently for me to finally get into a situation in which I would cry out to Him, and cry out I did.

I had married for the second time in 1977, this time to a Mormon. Stupid me, I didn't know that Mormonism was such an evil cult. I suffered much because of this ignorance. This went on until one day in 1978 when my neighbors reached out to me, inviting me to attend an Assembly of God church. By that time, my husband and I had a daughter, Kelly, who was then seven months old. I took Kelly with me, and we started attending that wonderful Spirit-filled church.

That year, 1978, around the spring, I gave my life and heart to the Lord Jesus Christ, and from that day on you could not keep me out of church. Every time the doors were open, I was there. Like a huge sponge, I was soaking everything up, learning about the Lord, studying His Word, attending a ladies' Bible study, learning how to walk with Jesus each and every day.

This radical change brought about a crisis in this second marriage. The day I got saved, I rushed home to tell my husband what had happened, but he didn't welcome this news. Instead, he immediately began planning his exit from the marriage. Here I was, a new mother with a beautiful daughter, and my husband was suddenly ready to walk out on both of us. I was devastated. I would quickly have to learn how to manage life with a small child, keep teaching school, and keep following the Lord. It would surely be a very difficult time for us.

I didn't give up on my marriage easily. I insisted on taking my husband to every Bible

How Did I Get So Far from God?

meeting I heard about, thinking that God would get hold of him too, but it was no use. He was solidly married to Mormonism and seemed to believe that if you left that cult, something bad would happen to you. As for me, my mind was made up. I could not turn back, and this he could not accept. The gulf between us widened.

I knew that God had a plan for my life, but Satan was trying his best to hinder it. As the struggles continued in our marriage, I began seeing visions in my room at night. In the first visions, legions of demons were advancing against me. I would cry out, "The blood of Jesus, the blood of Jesus," and they would immediately depart. This went on for two or three weeks before I could get a handle on what it was all about. Satan was determined to destroy me, but I was determined to stand fast.

My Mormon husband finally left. I guess he could not take the presence of the Holy Spirit. God had baptized me in the Holy Ghost with the evidence of speaking in my prayer language, and boy did I ever speak that prayer language. I did it all day long. And I still do it today after so many years. It is God's way of building us up.

During that time, I also learned about Free Masonry, another cult, somehow tied to Mormonism. Ladies, be careful who you date and who takes you to their church. The Lord had to pull me out of these ungodly cults.

At first, I had thought being a Mormon was like being a Baptist, just stricter. But, no, being a Mormon is nothing like being a Baptist. Mormonism is Satan's workshop. If you are hearing about this for the first time, please do your own research. Then, take a stand for the Lord Jesus Christ and stay away from Mormonism or any other cult. If any church's teaching does not line up with the Bible, RUN FROM IT as fast as you can.

Read the last chapter of the book of Revelation. The Lord is warning us through His Word, the Holy Bible. This is His love letter to us. Oh, He loves us so much, so very much!

If you are involved in a cult, you might have to change locations, and you might have to change friends. Whatever you have to do, get out of there as quickly as you possibly can.

During the years I was a single mom, I had many miracles take place. Money was tight.

How Did I Get So Far from God?

Mom and Daddy helped me tremendously, and I had great friends at the school where I taught. With everything, I always managed to take Kelly on a vacation to Florida with a wonderful friend, Diane Lovitz and her daughter, Kerry Lovitz. The memories we made with them were wonderful, and I am so thankful for their friendship during those difficult times.

Ladies, when trouble comes, don't think for a moment that your life is over. Rejoice that you have been set free and that we have a God who sees the beginning from the end. He takes care of the widows and orphans, and I am living proof of His never-failing love.

Being in a cult is total bondage. This particular cult, in my way of thinking, hates strong women. They want their women to stay at home and do nothing but cook, clean, and sew and service their men. Forget about having a life of your own or having your own thoughts and plans. They want total control of your mind, and that is evil. This is a very dangerous way to live, for you and for your children.

A Love Letter to God

Looking back, I can see that God saved me and my daughter, rescuing us out of that horrible pit. May all the glory be to Jesus.

At the same time, I have to admit that I got myself into that whole mess by being rebellious. Somehow I didn't understand what that word, *rebellion*, really meant. I see now that our family tribe on my mother's side was quite rebellious. It took years for me to break off the generational curses placed on us generations back in her family. Together, I and my blood sister have broken those curses, and we now walk in the blessings of the Lord. Praise His name!

This is something you might venture into when you are faced with these same issues. Check into your family line and see if there are any generational sins that have not been dealt with. I am now under the blood of Jesus Christ of Nazareth, and I bind the enemy off of me and my family. It has taken me years to gain perfect victory. Maybe I'm a slow learner, but others have helped me release these curses, and we are now seeing awesome blessings come into our family line.

My most important spiritual fathers have been Derek Prince, David Wilkerson, and John Hagee.

How Did I Get So Far from God?

There have been others, but these three men saved me from a life of misery. Billye Brimm is wonderful too. She has taught me a lot about generational curses and how to be set free from them.

You must come to the point that you really want to be set free from any bondage on yourself, your children, or anyone else in your family. When that moment comes, God will do it for you.

After being single again for six or seven years, during which time I prayed for a wonderful, loving, and sweet husband, I met my third husband—Craig Albert Owen—on a blind date. My friends were always looking out for me. Craig and I were married seven months later, after dating and making sure our plans were from God. Craig loved me and my daughter and took very good care of us, and I loved his daughter as well. I thank God that both our daughters are now grown, have married, and are very successful. I am so proud of them.

Craig, my precious husband, moved to Heaven in 2017. We were married for twenty-eight years, having married in 1990. There is a rainbow on the other end of every tragedy … if we will just cry out to God for help. When we call, He comes running to help us and our children, but He also demands that we be obedient to His calling for us and follow Him and His plan for our lives. I would not say that's always easy, but with Christ, all things are possible.

You have to put yourself and your family under the blood of Jesus and study the Word of God each day. I have not always been faithful in this regard, but I'm learning each day to stay pure and holy and to stay alert to God's call on my life. If we stay in church and faithfully tithe, then we can stand back and watch God move mountains.

How about you? Are you ready for a positive change in your life? Do you drink? Do you sleep around? Do you do drugs? Well, honey, get ready for a huge change. If you want to be whole and have a good life, you will have to renounce these things, stay away from fortune tellers, stay far away from tarot cards and people trying to read your fortune. These are of the devil. This is Satan's workshop, and he is trying to destroy your life. But, he can't win. He has already been defeated at the cross of Christ.

How Did I Get So Far from God?

Come to Jesus now. Come, and be set free from sin. You will be so happy, and you will be headed to Heaven one day when the Lord calls you home. Glory to God in the highest!

Just open your mouth now and ask Jesus to come into your life, forgive your sins, and make you whole. He will do it, but He wants you to come to Him and let Him control your life—what you do, where you live, even the friends you keep. You might have to walk away from people who have been keeping you trapped in sinful ways. I did.

Once I got saved, I lost a whole bunch of friends and even some family members. But, I count it all joy. I will never go back to being the rebellious person I was. Never!

Even if you are in a church, if you feel trapped by some ungodly thinking, just get out of it and go find a church that preaches the whole Word of God, a church that preaches the gifts of the Holy Spirit. These gifts are still in operation today. Become discerning.

Oh, by the way, God hates religion. Jesus is not religious. He is our King and Master and Savior. He came to set the captives free. And what He sets free is free indeed. Glory to God!

A Love Letter to God

Now, study the Word for yourself. Get with a friend or friends and meet each week for a Bible study. And ask the Lord for His help. He will lead you. Glory to God!

At one point, the Lord graciously started letting me sing for Bible studies, weddings, and funerals. I had always loved to sing, but now He took me up on my offer and gave me this assignment. I don't even read music, but I keep getting asked to sing. So, there is something about my voice that draws people. I have given my voice to the Lord to do with it as He wishes, and He has done wonders in this regard.

Back in the early 1980s I was called upon to sing for the Exchange Club in Houston. They would fly me to their National Meetings across the country. I only sang one song, the National Anthem, but I loved every minute of it. I am extremely patriotic, as they are.

Let us agree together that you are going to be used by the Lord too, when you have given yourself totally to Jesus Christ. He will make a way where there seems to be no way. Let us agree, once again, in prayer. You are reading this

How Did I Get So Far from God?

at the right time in your life, and God is getting you ready for your next adventure. It might be having a cooking show on TV or a new business idea. He knows your needs, and He loves to bless you. He loves to bless all His kids, and that includes you and me.

Stay away from alcohol and anyone who drinks. That is what I call a spirit of intoxication. It has destroyed so many children and families. Stay clean before the Lord, and you will be so glad you did. Welcome to your new life in Christ!

Chapter 2

Bad Choices Turned Around

Once I began to walk with the Lord, I started realizing just how bad my choices had been before. And I thought at the time that I was living a good, decent life! How sad!

Trying to stay up with the Joneses and have all the nice things in this world somehow never made me happy. Never! Over the years, Craig and I had five homes, and we moved often. We built four of those homes, but still, something was missing. I could have had five Mercedes, and that would not have made me happy. I knew I needed more in my life, and I discovered that what was missing was a close relationship with the Lord Jesus Christ.

Bad Choices Turned Around

I had to learn how to read the Word every day, stay connected with a Bible study and friends, and pray for my family and their needs and even their salvation. This has proved to be truly satisfying.

As much as Craig and I loved each other, he was very often off playing golf somewhere. He was an incredible golfer. Friends here in San Antonio told me they had never seen anyone with the kind of swing Craig had and not be a professional.

It was great to hear those things, but I was always being left alone. I didn't play golf with Craig because he was too good. So he played golf, and I concentrated on my Bible studies.

We did travel together. For instance, I accompanied him to New York City. There I prayed over all the bridges and walked the beautiful streets down by Radio City Music Hall and just prayed for the people I saw. Through the years, I learned to intercede for others.

I prayed for Donald J. Trump long before he was running for President. For some reason, I never prayed for Barack Obama. I'm so sorry, but I just didn't. I knew by the Spirit that something was not right with that man, and when they shined the rainbow lights on the White House, I fell to my knees and cried out to God to please intervene in the evil I saw developing before my eyes.

I also learned how to talk to people and tell them the truth. I had always been very shy and quiet, but after I received the Holy Ghost, something in me rose up, and I began to proclaim the Lord to everyone I met. I'm sure this made some people uneasy, but I didn't care. I cared more about their souls.

No one had told me about the Lord until I started visiting my neighbors in Missouri City, Texas. They had just been born again a year before me, and they were the only ones to tell me about Jesus and about how evil Mormonism was. No one else reached out to me like that couple, Bobby and Sandra Daileya. I am forever grateful that someone had the courage to tell me about the Lord, the true Jesus Christ, and not fake it like the Mormons.

When Christ came into my heart, my whole being changed. I suddenly cared about people and their personal prayer needs. I would go to Bible studies and take down the names of anyone who

Bad Choices Turned Around

needed prayer. I thought this was what everyone did, but later I learned that it wasn't always so. This was something unique. I was an intercessor.

For a while, I didn't understand what being an intercessor meant, but I soon found out. Often I could not fall asleep at night until I had prayed for the people God was laying on my heart. He gave me their names, and I stayed up at all hours of the night to intercede for them. That is how intercession worked in my life. Someone had interceded for me, and now I was interceding for others the Lord brought to my attention.

In my sleep, the Lord showed me parts of New York that were being targeted by terrorists, and I would wake up as if I had some sort of radar and intercede for those places. Something horrible had been planned, but my prayers and the prayers of others stopped it. We may not know until we get to Heaven all that our prayers have accomplished, but I am honored to pray. I truly am. In fact, I find it to be a lot of fun praying for other people and their needs.

When I'm home by myself interceding for those the Lord places on my heart, I often cry like a baby, but being a prayer warrior and an intercessor is my greatest joy, along with teaching little children.

A funny incident happened while we were living in Bellaire, Texas. Craig and I had just built a huge home, way too big for the two of us, but we moved into it anyway. We kept that home for several years.

Bellaire is a small but interesting community. It is made up of some medium-sized homes, but they were tearing down older homes and building huge homes in their place. Our was one of those.

I enjoyed decorating the house, but the house itself did not make me happy. Craig was a money manager, and the market was up some years and then down the next, so I learned a serious lesson: live within your means.

At one point, early in the years of the new century, we had to move into a rental home because Craig had to declare bankruptcy. I was happy in that rental home, and it was comfortable, even though I had a long drive to and from work—fifty miles each way. With taking care of my parents at the same time, that was quite a challenge.

Bad Choices Turned Around

For some reason, we kept running into some Muslim men in our community—at the store, at the coffee shop, at the post office, etc. I got a funny feeling being around them, but somehow it seems they got the idea that I was some sort of spy. No kidding. I did sense in the Spirit what they were up to, and it was not good. One day the Holy Spirit showed me that they were planning an invasion that would begin with bringing down a huge office building around the Galleria area. I never told this to anyone before. What should I do?

One day, when I went to Starbucks to get a cup of coffee, I asked the Lord to let me bump into them and to have some fun with them. When I saw them, I held my cellphone to my ear as if I were talking to someone and started speaking in my prayer language. One of the men heard me. He tapped me on the shoulder and said, "Hey, I hear you speaking Arabic."

I said, "Oh, yes, I speak a little Arabic." Of course, I didn't speak any Arabic, but boy did I have fun with them that day. I later rejoiced, knowing that I had been speaking in Arabic in the Spirit. I have no idea what I said that day, but whatever it was caused those men to leave town. We never saw them again. You can't outdo the Holy Ghost.

When we love the Lord and follow His ways, He gives us such joy. This is true even when we might be having our own issues—money issues, health issues, or whatever. The key, for me, is to keep praising the Lord no matter what comes.

Craig and I got through the bankruptcy, and we ended up with two more beautiful homes in the New Braunfels and San Antonio area. God is a Restorer. He restores what the locusts have eaten. He is all about restoration, the restoration of broken relationships, broken homes, and broken hearts. He can work His magic on anything that's broken. He is so wonderful. I will praise Him every day as long as I have breath. I thank God that I can pray and walk with Him each day. Glory to His matchless name!

Chapter 3

Jesus Came into My Bedroom

I had never had such a thing happen before, but this time it did. I was recovering from knee surgery in 2011. Craig had suffered a mild stroke earlier that year, and with everything I seemed to be very stressed out. I was crying out to the Lord, asking Him to please come into my bedroom and show me that He was real. Well, ladies and gentlemen, that is exactly what He did.

I was lying in bed in a room at the opposite side of the house because Craig had a breathing issue that often kept me awake. It was a beautiful bedroom, a perfect place for me to recover from the surgery. I was only half awake, but what happened next was not a dream, and it was not a vision. This was real. This was a visitation from the Lord Himself.

Jesus walked through the door into my bedroom, and I suddenly found myself looking right into His beautiful eyes. Oh, my goodness, words cannot possibly describe my joy at that moment. The joy of the Lord was all over me.

What happened next was again shocking. He came near and hugged me. He actually hugged me, and you should have seen me hug Him back.

All the time Jesus was with me, He didn't utter a word, and yet He let me know how much He loved me. He didn't stay long, maybe five or ten minutes, and when He left I fell back into my bed, bawling like a baby. When I was finally able to compose myself, I ran as fast as I could with my new knee and told Craig what had just happened.

Before, when I heard anyone talking about a visitation from the Lord, I couldn't identify with what they were saying. Now I understood. Now I believed. It had happened to me too.

Somehow I can still see Him. He is beautiful. He's almost six feet tall, He's thin, He has a beard, and He is wearing some sort of gown. I

Jesus Came into My Bedroom

know this may be hard for some to believe, but all I can do is share with you what happened to me and how amazing it was. That experience was so powerful that it changed me completely.

His eyes are incredible. I still see them today. Don't let anyone tell you that He's not real.

God's Word tells us that in the latter days He will pour out His Spirit on all mankind, and we will experience dreams, visions, and miracles. I have seen Jesus, and I know what He says is real.

My daughter received the Holy Ghost at John Osteen's church sometime in the late 1990s and spoke in her prayer language. That experience totally changed her life. It was such a miracle that even Craig noticed the difference in her. She was a new woman. She even smelled like roses. We serve a wonderful, miraculous God. Don't let anyone ever tell you that He no longer does miracles.

I had another visitation years before, but it was an open vision. I was with my oldest brother. He was dressed in a beautiful tuxedo, and I was dressed in a gorgeous long gown with diamonds across the front of it. I wish I could draw it like I saw it that day because that gown was, as they say, "out of this world."

We were getting ready for a great feast, and there were others in a huge ballroom. I came to the conclusion that it must have been the Wedding Supper of the Lamb. When searching the Scriptures, I found a portion that speaks of that great day coming in the near future.

I had been praying for my precious brother for years, so I know he had made it to Heaven. I knew that by the Spirit of God. Never stop praying for your siblings, your other loved ones, your friends, and also your enemies. Keep praying for them, keep loving them, and keep short accounts.

We have all been hurt by words from the mouths of others, and we have hurt others with our words. If we are the offender, we must repent and move on. If we are the offended, God will take care of it for us.

I have learned to be careful what I pray for, as I just might get my prayer request. Never pray for someone to die or to be murdered, even if they have hurt you. Never pray for their demise. Just move on and do your best and keep praising the

Jesus Came into My Bedroom

Lord. Forgive, forgive, forgive, and forgive some more. That will keep your soul healthy.

I have learned in my own life to keep short accounts. God keeps us in the palm of His hands, and He forgets our past. He says that He puts our failings in the sea of forgetfulness. What a strong promise! Be like Jesus and do the same for others.

We have much to pray about in our country. So many of our leaders have neglected God in their personal lives. But God will deal with them, not you or me. Let Him do what He does best. Personally, I fear the Lord. I really do, in a healthy way, and don't want anything to hinder my relationship with Him ever. Heaven is too good to miss.

Chapter 4

Not My Will, but Thine Be Done

When I began this walk of mine with the Lord, I learned a truth that I shall never ever forget: no matter how old we are in the Lord, we are all still learning. We're all still in school, so to speak. I call it THE SCHOOL OF THE HOLY SPIRIT.

Only God's Spirit can adequately direct our path toward Jesus Christ and His righteousness. I want to live a good life, a life filled with fun and adventure, but also I want a life with Jesus as my Pilot. As Jesus prayed, "Not my will, but Thy will be done" in my life.

Beloved, if you are reading this today, don't hesitate to stop and give your life to God right

Not My Will, but Thine Be Done

now. Ask Him to come in and take control of your life—your family, your job, your work, your play. This will be the best decision you have ever made. Relationships will begin to change for you. You will be set free from the past and from hurts you may have been carrying for decades. Life is to be enjoyed; it should not be a burden or a binding.

I lived with a lot of fear before asking the Lord into my life, and maybe you have too. Today, I know beyond a shadow of a doubt that my life is better than it has ever been. Challenges have come, but God has promised to deliver us out of them all. We might have to go through some pretty hairy things while down here on planet Earth, but beloved, never give up on Jesus Christ. May the Lord honor and bless your going in and coming out. May He be the shining Light in your life and the life of your family. We can't lose with Jesus on our side. Praise His name forever and ever.

Chapter 5

Being Sidelined for Years on End

During those years I was raising my daughter alone, being sidelined took its toll on me. I was running out of money and needed a new plan for raising Kelly. But God heard my cries. In early 1989, my parents invited Kelly and me to come live with them for a time. This turned out to be the best thing that could have happened to us.

Kelly's dad had left me with nothing, absolutely nothing, but I got the best part of the deal. I got Kelly, and that was worth all the gold in the world. I got my beautiful daughter. Praise the Lord!

Being Sidelined for Years on End

I worried about Kelly because she had seen many women come and go in her dad's life. This was quite upsetting for me too, but what could I do? Kelly definitely needed a change.

When we went to live with Mom and Daddy, I got a job teaching fourth grade in a little country school, and I put Kelly in sixth grade at the same school. What a blessing this turned out to be! She flourished there and made straight A's. I was so proud of her. She became very strong in her beliefs too, and she knew the Lord.

Craig and I began dating in 1989, just a week after I had moved to Conroe, Texas. By Christmas we were engaged to be married, and the following St. Patrick's day, we officially tied the knot. We had a glorious honeymoon in Banff, Canada, Mom and Daddy took good care of Kelly while we honeymooned, and right after that, we moved back to Houston.

Kelly stayed with my parents and finished sixth grade, and then we moved together to our first beautiful home in Bellaire, Texas. There the Lord opened the door for us to put Kelly in a private school. I was so thankful because she got a great education in a Lutheran high school in Houston. She then went on to the university and graduated with all A's and B's. Life was beginning to turn around for us all, and I had the family I had always dreamed of.

I also have to confess that there were times when I had lost hope of ever seeing help come our way. Then, when Craig was forced into bankruptcy, it rocked our world again. But we managed beautifully. God was taking care of all three of us.

About this time, Mom and Daddy were slowly on the decline, and all six of us kids pitched in to help them get through it. It wasn't easy. Growing up, we had always been a very close-knit clan, and anytime you have to hire caregivers to come into your home, it produces a lot of anger, sadness, and just plain not knowing what to do next. But we got through it.

My oldest brother was great. He was the executor of my parents' estate, and he did a great job. Daddy passed first in 2010, and Mom followed in 2013. They were believers, so we know we would see them again. All of our believing relatives are rejoicing together in Heaven awaiting our great graduation

Being Sidelined for Years on End

day, and it's coming soon, very soon, I do believe.

I believe in the Rapture of the Church and am very adamant about it. Read the Word for yourself. Read 1st and 2nd Thessalonians. These books tell us what's next on God's agenda. There are many varied interpretations of these sacred writings, but it seems very clear to me that it will all happen very soon. After all, the signs we were told to look for have appeared.

Do your own research on this subject. Read the book of Revelation. It explains it all. There is a huge blessing awaiting those of us who will sit down and take the time to read God's Word every day.

When I started reading the book of Revelation, at first it seemed very strange, but I persisted because I wanted to know the truth. It was not long after I got saved in 1978 that I started reading it, and I was deeply touched by what the Lord was about to do. That knowledge kept me going.

From that time on, I have read the Word every day. I was always in a Bible study and still am. Now, however, I read it on my own and do a lot of praying for people. God loves people, and

A Love Letter to God

if you don't love people, something is wrong. Check with God. He will give you supernatural love for people you might not even like. I have surely had some rough people I had to deal with, but I just pray for them, ask the Lord to bless them, and I move on. I refuse to dwell on what they may have done to me. It's not worth going to Hell over. *"Vengeance is mine, saith the Lord."*

I love reading the Old Testament. Those prophets knew what they were talking about, and they're still speaking to us today. Read their words. That will wake you up. Don't let anyone tell you not to read the Old Testament. Read it for yourself, do your own research, and pray as you read it. Ask the Holy Spirit to open your spiritual eyes and ears to what is about to happen. Glory to God, we get to go Home, and Home is forever.

Either you give your life to the Lord and go to Heaven, or you ignore Him and end up in Hell. Hell is a very real place, and there are no weekend visits. Once you are there, you are there forever. Think about it! I can't even imagine how awful that place must be. But you can avoid it. You still have a choice. Choose the God of the Bible.

Being Sidelined for Years on End

Check out all the people who have had dreams and visions of Hell. My God, it is horrible! On the other hand, Heaven is so wonderful. It is full of love and peace and grandeur. Many have had dreams and visions of Heaven. I sure have, and what I have seen blows me away. I can't stop crying. The Lord Jesus Christ is so real. Never ever let anyone tell you any different.

Heaven is where you want to go, not Hell. Get rid of your rebellion, and ask the Lord to show you what Heaven is like. Keep asking Him and keep trusting Him. You will be in the battle of your life, but with the Word of God as your sword, you will win this battle. The Word of God is your Sword (see Ephesians 6), and so God gets all the glory.

Chapter 6

On My Way to Heaven

By God's grace, I am on my way to Heaven. Are you? Have you made a profession of faith in the Lord Jesus Christ? This is the most important decision you will ever make in life.

I make mistakes every day. Of course I do. I'm human. Now I see life through a different lens. I see with my spiritual eyes and hear with my spiritual ears because I chose to become a child of God.

This is all very supernatural. Please don't be afraid of that word *supernatural*. A lot of so-called religious folks are so afraid of stepping into error that they throw the gifts of the Holy Spirit down the drain. Well, I have embraced everything the Lord has for me.

On My Way to Heaven

Now I see how Jesus must have felt when He walked the Earth, trying to finish the assignment Father God had given Him down here—to save us from ourselves, to save us from Hell. A literal Hell awaits Satan's angels and those he brings with him down to the Pit. Please don't let this be your fate.

Jesus asked me to become His child, and I took Him up on His offer. It was free. You don't have to pay anything to join His family.

God is all about family, so just be yourself and ask the Lord Jesus into your life. Repent of your sins and ask Him to forgive you of those sins. He will make you a child of God. How? He will change you from the inside out. I have never been happy just to be a pew-sitter. I want God's Word to be alive in me every day. You and I can spread the Good News by telling others about what God has done in our lives and living it out before them.

As a believer in Christ, you must trust Him with your life. Trust Him for your future and do things God's way. That is the key to the mind change we get when we're saved. You have to trust God to prove Himself to you every single day.

A Love Letter to God

I wish you the most wonderful life in the Holy Spirit as you begin your new existence. If you let Him, the Lord will take away anger, He will take away bad friends, and He will take away bad business decisions. He will give you the courage to walk through fire, and He will give you opportunities that may be totally new to you.

God gives His people witty inventions. He gives us visions and dreams and does daily miracles to move us forward into the things He has prepared for us. I wish you a most blessed life. Just be sure not to miss Him. Don't miss the opportunity to be saved and filled with the Holy Spirit.

Our God is a no-nonsense God. He is wonderful. He is my Best Friend, and He will be your Best Friend too. He gets all the glory. He does not share His glory with anyone else. He is the Ruler of the Universe, and He is Sovereign, always and forever.

At the end of this book, I have written several scriptures that have spoken to me during the time I was writing. I was the last person to ever think I could sit down and write my story. It has been an adventure of the highest magnitude.

On My Way to Heaven

We are all on a journey, and your journey is as important as mine.

You, too, have something to say. Write it down, pray over it, cry over it, intercede for your book too. God has people waiting for you to speak to about your personal journey.

If you are a believer in Christ, you and I are about to experience the most wonderful day of our lives—the Rapture of the Church. It will happen in God's perfect timing. He has His own calendar. Check it out for yourself. Do your own research.

Souls are waiting to be saved, and it could come from what you say to one person, maybe over a cup of coffee or a nice dinner, just the two of you. God knows your heart. May God's blessings be upon each and every one of you as you read this story of love, heartache, mystery, and hardship. In the end, it all seems worth it to me.

Whatever you do, don't let Satan steal your joy. He has come to kill, steal, and destroy you as best as he can. Close every door to the enemy and welcome the Holy Spirit into your life, and He will lead you into joy and wonderful adventures. Yes, the best is yet to come.

Just ask my friend, Steve Schultz. He was instrumental in me coming to the realization of the prophetic in my life. This started around the beginning of his wonderful ministry when I got to see him minister in 1984 or 1985. Steve and his lovely wife Derene started me on this incredible journey. Thank you, Steve and Derene. God's blessing be upon you and all your wonderful media sites. You have given so many an opportunity to express their own ministries. We are all in the family of God. Glory be to our great King!

Chapter 7

My First Vision

I received the Lord in 1978, and I want to recount the very first vision I received. I was so young in the Lord I didn't know what a vision was. Through the years, I have had many visions, but this was the first.

It was an open vision. I was awake and had asked the Lord a question, if the Rapture was really going to take place in my lifetime. That was all I asked, but what He showed me blew me away.

I was lying in bed, when suddenly the room went dark, and I began to see unusual things. It was all in color. I was so startled that I jumped to my feet. I saw the world in travail. It reminded me of a woman about to give birth.

A Love Letter to God

As I stood there mesmerized, a picture of a man appeared. I wasn't able to see his face, but he suddenly turned into a skeleton. I was in shock.

My husband was lying there in bed, and I tried to tell him what was happening. Then I left the room and went to sit in the living room to pray. I asked the Lord what it all meant, and He answered to my satisfaction.

Never make fun of someone's visions or dreams. God gives each of us a piece of the puzzle. He uses people to spread His Word, and He is preparing us for what is coming. When will it all happen? God has a totally different time clock than ours. He knows all things.

The Lord took Jessie Duplantis to Heaven while he was in a hotel room, and he was in Heaven for about four hours. What he came back, he shared with us what he had seen. I love to hear him on TV.

Many others in the Body of Christ have had and are still having dreams and visions today. This was not just for the Old Testament prophets. It's still happening. Jesus is real, and His Word is powerful and true.

My First Vision

My prayer times are very important to me. The longer I pray, the more God shows me. He said, *"Call unto me, and I will answer thee, and show thee great and mighty things, which thou knowest not"* (Jeremiah 33:3). I will never stop seeking Him.

Because I know what it is to be lost, my heart is for the lost. Yes, I was once lost, but now I'm found. Glory to God! Believe God for your family and friends to know the Lord, to come to the saving knowledge of Jesus Christ. Because of your testimony, they will have their own testimony one day.

My goal is to keep doing what the Lord has called me to do, and that is praying for the lost, praying for children who have horrible home lives, and helping them in any way I can to be delivered from those situations.

As a teacher for over twenty-five years, I have known many different children, and many of them came from very troubled home situations. On one occasion, I went to court to testify that one of my fourth-grade students was being sexually abused by her father. She kept trying to tell her teachers over the years, but no one would listen. When I heard her situation, I said, "Okay, this stops here and now."

A Love Letter to God

I testified for more than an hour. As a result, that child was removed from her home and placed in a more stable atmosphere. Sadly, the father only got probation. I always wondered what happened to Barbara. She was such a sweet little girl, and it literally made me sick to hear what her father was doing to her. I was only too glad to stand up for her, and I never regretted it. I prayed that she would be safe and find a good family. She is now a grown woman.

Teachers need to be willing to take a chance and get out of their comfort zone to help needy students and save them from horrific situations.

Satan is real too, and he comes to kill, steal, and destroy. Get your life right with the Lord. Jesus trumps them all, and all the evil will cease to exist once we get to Heaven. Delight yourself in the things of the Lord, pray for your family members, and don't stop praying until they are safely in God's fold.

Listen to your children and ask them pertinent questions. Who are they hanging out with? Make sure they are safe around other grownups, and with the Lord's help, remain alert at all times for danger for their sake. This includes in and out of

My First Vision

church, at ballgames, ballet and tap classes, etc. Bad things can happen in any situation.

As you get your life lined up with the King of Kings and see to it that your children do the same, it will be worth all your hard work.

Many prophets and many ordinary people, like myself, are beginning to speak out. I will keep singing, speaking, and sharing the Good News of God as long as I have my health, and I fully intend to keep my eyes on the Lord. That is a worthy goal for all of us.

Sometimes I don't fall asleep until about three or four in the morning, but I still wake up early and have a great day because God keeps me going. He has called me to pray and intercede for others. Be alert to His still small voice to know His will for your life.

Chapter 8

What Do You Want to Get out of the Bible?

"Life, liberty, and the pursuit of happiness." Our country was founded upon the Bible, and God has a plan for you and for me, for our families, and for our country. Stand strong for the United States of America. We must bring God back into our schools and bring prayer back too. Maybe the Lord is speaking to you to do something toward that end. He will reward us all for any effort we make for Him.

Thank you, Brother Steve Schultz, for being the very first person to introduce me to the wonderful atmosphere of the Holy Spirit and to help me listen to the Lord's voice. I will be

What Do You Want to Get out of the Bible?

forever grateful. We met in Corpus Christi at a Christian conference in 1984 or 1985. God bless his websites, and God bless the many witty inventions the Lord is giving him and his wife and family. This is all in the realm of the Spirit. I want to make a difference here too. This is my first attempt at writing what has happened to me. Thank you, Steve, for helping me with this. I am grateful.

I pray no cult will invade your life or the lives of your children and grandchildren. Speak to them. Do not allow Satan to invade their lives. Jesus wants to save us all. He loves people, and He is absolutely good all the time.

I am learning more each day about the Word of God and the Lord Himself. Learn to study His Word. He is powerful. Talk to Him. Ask Him questions. Get with Him in your private time and spend time with Him. Praise Him. He inhabits the praises of His people always and forever.

My favorite Scripture verses are listed at the end of this book. As I mentioned in an earlier chapter, I started reading the book of Revelation as a young Christian. I wanted to know the end

A Love Letter to God

from the beginning. Born in 1948, I am now seventy-seven years old.

Something very important happened in 1948: Israel became a nation. That was key. Follow the feasts of Israel. They are key. Our Jesus is Jewish, and I have fallen in love with my Jewish Messiah.

Some of the ministers I personally follow are: Billye Brimm, Carolyn Sissom, John Hagee, Derek Prince, David Wilkerson, Sid Roth, Robin Bullock, Steve Schultz, Bill and Jane Hamon, Charlie Shamp and others. I will be forever grateful to all the wonderful friends and mentors who have helped me on my way to learn about how to walk in the Spirit, how to study the Word of God, and how to live in the joy of the Lord, no matter what is going on around me. Whatever season I happen to be in, God is with me every day of this incredible journey.

Get ready for what is about to take place on Planet Earth. God said we would know the season, know about the time things would take place. He certainly knows, and when the Rapture of the Church takes place, we will all go home to spend eternity with our King, Jesus

What Do You Want to Get out of the Bible?

Christ of Nazareth. Those of us wo are Christians now walk in the Kingdom of God, no longer in the kingdom of darkness here on the Earth. We are citizens of a very different Kingdom, a righteous Kingdom. Thank God for that!

Chapter 9

The First True Miracle

The first true miracle that took place in my life is that I was able to escape a life of misery as a Mormon wife. Oh, thanks be to God. I had the good sense to ask the Lord about what Mormonism was, and when He showed me, I got out of it.

Mormons may look good on the outside, happy and normal. But believe me, they're not. Beware of anyone pretending to be godly. Why would my Mormon husband leave our marriage? After all, I had been obedient to take the lessons to join the Mormon church. I did what he asked me to do. Was he afraid of what I had learned? I will never know, but I had the good sense to ask the Lord of Lords, Jesus Christ, if that religion was

The First True Miracle

really from God. The Lord answered me while I was standing in the doorway of my bedroom. He said very clearly, "Helen, this is not of me."

I wasn't sure God was doing the talking, but I started researching Mormonism and was shocked to learn what they really believed in and required of their members. It was horrible.

Have you seen the movie, "The Stepford Wives"? There have been several versions of it through the years. I remembered seeing it years before, and that memory hastened my decision to jump at the opportunity the Lord was giving me to make my escape from this devilish cult.

It took me several more years to finally divorce my Mormon husband. I hated divorce, and God hates divorce too, but this was not the life God wanted for me and my beautiful daughter.

I am sure Kelly has her own memories of this time as a small child. She has grown into a beautiful young woman and has given me four precious grandsons. One day, when they get older, they will be asking her about her biological father. I pray that they will never get involved with their grandfather's cult.

A Love Letter to God

There are many false cults at work in our world today. Be careful what you walk into, beloved. You have to do your own research. Remember to ask questions and keep asking questions. Talk to your children about the dangers of false cults. Spend time in the Word of God with them. Do not let them be deceived like I was.

When I came to myself and began to ask questions, wanting to get to the truth of a matter, my husband immediately wanted out of the marriage and started dating other women. He had become a very successful stockbroker in Houston, and he was hiding his money from me and our daughter. I never knew who he was seeing or what he was doing. He was very secretive. But looking back on it, I can see that God provided our every need His way. He is our Provider, He is our Great Physician, He is our Everything … if we will just trust Him for all our needs and wants.

A person can do evil to others, but it will always be exposed in God's timing. And, in the meantime, He will make a way for His people.

Now angels began appearing to me in various situations. I had never thought that angels were

The First True Miracle

real, but they are. Later God showed me in the Scriptures the many times angels had intervened in the lives of the saints. They appear when needed to this very day, but you have to be very discerning. Ask the Lord if angels are from Him or from the devil and search the Scriptures for yourself. Don't just take my word for it. Trust the Lord and His Word. Spend time with Him. Don't rely on the word of others.

I taught school during this whole time of testing and growth (or whatever you want to call it), and it has made me into a strong woman of God. The best part about this time was I was learning the Word of God and learning about people. If it took me being married to a Mormon to bring me to that, then so be it. What a school of learning this turned out to be for me and my daughter! No one can possibly understand the depths of evil until they walk in it themselves.

Be very careful who you criticize. You don't know what that person has gone through unless you have walked a mile in their shoes. I have learned to be very careful what comes out of my mouth. I am human and have said things I shouldn't have, but I am much more discerning these days. I don't tell many people everything that happened to me, how I literally had to fight for my life during this time.

One evening we went to a restaurant, and I somehow was poisoned. I could feel that something was not right, and by the time we got home, my face was horribly swollen. I had never seen such a thing and begged my husband to take me to the ER, but he refused.

That night, I felt like I was dying. I cried out to God, and eventually I heard an angel interceding (I believe it was Michael). He was fighting off the demons. I actually heard fist-fighting in the Spirit. I either fell asleep or passed out, and when I woke up I had been in bed for two days.

I was finally able to drive myself to the doctor, and he said to me, "Helen, you have been poisoned." Poisoned? I couldn't understand that. I will probably never know the whole story, but whatever happened, God brought me through it, with that angel fighting off a legion of demons.

When I first got saved and filled with the Holy Spirit, I would see these demons coming after me. I know this sounds like I'm "nuts," but I know what I saw. The only thing that would

The First True Miracle

make them leave me alone was to say, "The blood of Jesus has saved me." I would say that four or five times, and they would disappear. I saw them and can describe what they looked like and what they had in their hands—swords. Once that Mormon husband left our home for good, I never saw those demons again.

After the divorce, Kelly and I were forced out of our home, but we found a cute little condo in Quail Valley and stayed there for next five years until I remarried. Thanks be to God that He had a plan for us, and He has plans for you and your children too, plans to bless you and prosper you. Do things God's way, and you will always be so glad you followed the Lord Jesus Christ, not the fake Jesus Mormonism follows. Their Jesus is a counterfeit.

My advice to women is to get out of a bad marriage, and get out of it as quickly as possible. Many bad marriages are hopeless. Get out. My husband refused to accept Jesus as His personal Lord and Savior, so I had no choice. I was not about to raise my daughter in a godless cult. Nor was I ever personally going to submit to such evil. As I have walked with the Lord, He has shown me so many miracles. My good friend Karen Bovett prayed for me all the time, and I will be forever grateful to her and her hours of praying and interceding for me and my beautiful daughter.

Get involved in a church that preaches the whole Word of God, not some milk toast gospel. God is the Author of our salvation and I truly believe He allowed me to go through all this so that I can help spread the Good News of the Gospel of Jesus Christ and His gifts in the Holy Spirit.

Some churches choose to ignore the book of Acts. I needed a Full Gospel church that truly taught how to be set free from any kind of demonic influence a person might have walked into. Thank God for Braeswood Assembly of God. That is where I was trained to learn about the Lord and His fullness. Steve Banning was our pastor at the time. I stayed there for five years.

Braeswood Assembly had a great Ladies' Bible Study, and that was how I got my training. And I stayed with it. I never departed from the faith or let go of God. I stayed right with Him through the good and the bad. I had made my decision

The First True Miracle

to follow Jesus, and I was not about to turn back.

Will you stay with Jesus too? Will you take the chance and let God be God in your life? The rewards are many.

I am now based in San Antonio, Texas and am a member of Cornerstone Church, the church John Hagee founded. I am thankful to God for his precious family that has truly and faithfully served the Lord. Now their son, Matt Hagee, is doing a marvelous job as pastor. May God bless this whole family.

Thank God we live in a free country where we can attend the church of our choice, that we don't live under Communist rule. That is something we definitely don't want for ourselves, our children, or our grandchildren. It's time to get back to the Bible.

I stopped watching the news, deciding that I would rather listen to godly men and women. I got rid of my cable TV because there was such trash on it. And God is doing a new work in my life. I am speaking more about what happened to me so many years ago, when I was first born again. Life is wonderful again.

Stay strong, my friend. Stand for truth, and fight the good fight of faith. We will win this battle together. Stay far away from alcohol and drugs, and away from anyone who tries to ruin your life or your children's lives.

Ask God to give you discernment about who you hang out with, both inside and outside of the church. Just because someone goes to church does not necessarily mean they're truly born again. Look what Jesus had to go through. Upon that cross, He gave His life for each and every one of us. Believe on the Lord Jesus Christ, accept His sacrifice, and you will be saved.

Chapter 10

Who Is Jesus?

As I was growing up in Port Arthur, Texas, I did attend church off and on—two churches as a matter of fact. Mom and Dad had made some sort of decision. We would attend Mom's Baptist church for the first ten years of our lives and then attend Dad's church, the Disciples of Christ. In all those years, however, I never learned a thing about the real Jesus. To me, it was all just a lot of baloney. All Jesus was to me at this time was just another person in a book, the Bible, and it made no sense to me at all.

Then, as a teenager, I got terribly sidetracked and fell into sin. Now, after making so many mistakes in relationships and being married three times, it makes one look back and say, "Jesus was real after all." It was in 1978 that I decided to give Him a chance in my life, and it was the best decision I could ever have made. I am so grateful.

Then, after two horrible marriages, God sent me Craig Albert Owen, my wonderful husband who loved me and loved my daughter as his own. He had his own daughter, Laura Owen, and I came to love her as well. I even came to love the family of Craig's first wife. God worked it all out for His glory.

Life was different now because after those first two horrible marriages, I found the Lord. Better said, He found me. I was a very lonely "messed up" young woman of twenty-nine when I got saved and baptized in the Holy Ghost at Braeswood Assembly of God under Pastor Earl Banning. As I mentioned in an earlier chapter, you could not keep me out of church. I was there every time the church doors were open. Every time they had a conference or a guest speaker, I was there.

I regularly attended the Ladies' Bible Study and began to read the Word of God for the first time in my life, and He changed me from the inside out. Praise God!

Who Is Jesus?

I used to hate that saying. That's how broken I was. But God healed me and delivered me from wrong thinking, wrong associations, and so much more. The Lord is wonderful, and He is real. I literally fell in love with Him. Today, the Lord is my heart. His love is amazing!

My life turned around when I received Jesus as my Lord and Savior, and then the baptism of the Holy Ghost changed my walk with the Lord. The power of the Holy Spirit is so transformational. I would need to write another book on all the miracles the Lord has performed in my life through the years.

I am now seventy-seven, and I pray that this short book will help you on your path to find the Lord and trust Him with your whole being. I pray that you will not make the same mistakes I made. I am no longer filled with pride and am grateful for this opportunity to share with you what God can do with a broken vessel. He can turn our ashes into gold.

The Lord has sent many wonderful Christian friends into my life, the first being Karen Bovett (Oh my God, what a wonderful and loving friend). Then there was Sister Carolyn Sissom, my Pastor at the Little White Church in Katy, Texas, and many other wonderful ladies helped me on this path.

As I have mentioned, Steve Schultz was the first man to show me the Lord. I met him in the early eighties at a conference he was involved in. The prophet who was speaking asked Steve something to the affect of: "Steve, who do you know here that you want me to prophesy over?" Steve spoke my name because I had been in touch with him a few months before. My memory of this moment just recently came back to me. I had asked the Holy Spirit to help me remember the details of that day. I couldn't even remember the name of the prophet who was speaking. He told me I would be writing a book, and it would be painful to write, but God would help me.

Write a book? I was a school teacher, but I was no book writer. This would be a "game changer" for me. That word stayed with me through the years until I finally dared to sit down and start writing. And, yes, it was painful, but as the prophet foretold, the Lord has helped me.

Who Is Jesus?

I am grateful to Steve for that conference and the sensitivity to know that God wanted to speak to me. Steve, God bless you and your awesome ministry to all of us who love and care for people and where they end up, either Heaven or Hell (God forbid).

Friend, give Jesus a chance in your life. Hell is real and you don't want to go there. Give Jesus Christ of Nazareth a fighting chance to reveal Himself to you. It doesn't matter if you're an MBA, a physicist, a doctor, a yardman, or a dishwasher. Jesus loves us all just the same. He is truly the first Person to show me love, just the way He made me. I am unorganized, energetic, and can't read a lick of music, but God has allowed me to sing for Him. And I love teaching little kids and helping them to grow up to be the best they can be for God. I just want to shine for Him. I want Him to be proud of me for turning my life around. It was my choice, and I chose life. I chose Jesus Christ.

It took me some years to understand God's love for me. I felt that I was not good enough for anyone to love. I was the oldest of six children, but, for some reason, I never felt quite good enough. But God had a plan for me. Keep seeking the truth, and never stop seeking the Lord. Truth can be found only in Him and His wonderful Word. You can trust Him.

Chapter 11

Listening to the Holy Spirit

This last chapter is very crucial to my story. Once you accept the Lord, wanting everything He has planned for you, you cannot avoid His Holy Spirit. The power to live the Christian life is to be found in the Holy Spirit, the third Person of the Trinity. He is God's representative here on the Earth, and He desires to bless you, your tribe, your business, your everything. But you have to be willing to listen to His counsel.

As you read the book of Acts, the history of the earliest days of the Church, you cannot but recognize the important place the Spirit played in the lives of those early saints. Amazingly, some very religious people have thrown out the book of Acts as not being relevant for today. But

A Love Letter to God

nothing could be more relevant! Without the Holy Spirit we are powerless.

My exciting life in Christ started when I found a wonderful church that taught Acts as a living book, our pattern for life and ministry today. There I was baptized in the Spirit, and the fireworks started going off in my walk with Jesus.

I sure made the devil angry. He did everything he could to frighten me away from this blessing, but when we stay prayed up, he has no power over us. Read the Psalms, read the Proverbs, and see how God delivered those who trusted Him from the evil one and his hideous plans.

Satan might know some things, but he surely doesn't know all the plans of God. He is out to kill, steal, and destroy your walk with Jesus, and he will go to any length to hurt you and your family and business. This is why it's important to put on the whole armor of God each morning as you wake up. Then stay girded with that armor as you gain victory after victory in your prayer life. Learn to walk in the Spirit.

God often wakes me up in the early hours of the morning. I ask Him, "Lord, who is it that You want me to pray for tonight?" On many days,

Listening to the Holy Spirit

the answer has been "President Trump and his family."

Not so long ago, I suffered a grand mal seizure right there in my doctor's office, and I didn't remember any of it. They rushed me by ambulance to the hospital. I had ignored the warning signs of my health. But, glory to God, I am now fine, am on the right meds, and have suffered no more seizures.

I was in the hospital for three days, and they ran all sorts of tests on me. What happened on the last day of my hospital visit changed my life, especially my prayer life. As I was lying there in the hospital bed, I asked the Lord, "Why didn't You just take me home to Heaven?" He answered so clearly:

HELEN, I BROUGHT YOU BACK TO PRAY FOR DONALD TRUMP!

There was also an angel who spoke to me. He was next to my right ear, and I heard him say, "You have lost relatives who need to be saved." I soon got out of that sick bed, my sister took me home, and I upped my prayer time for Donald

J. Trump and his family and for all my unsaved loved ones and friends. God knows their hearts, but my assignment in this hour is to pray like I have never done before.

In one of Perry Stone's videos, he spoke of his father, an amazing man of God, saying that in the last days we would have to pray in the Spirit more than ever. I believe that. Thank you, Brother Perry, for sharing those words. That is the truth. This is not milk toast time; THIS IS WAR! Stand up, put on your battle fatigues, cover yourself in the blood of the Lamb, read Your Sword (the Bible), and be ready in season and out of season.

Saints, we must stand for righteousness as never before. I am pro-life, I am pro-Trump, and I am pro-America. Anyone who believes in slaughtering little babies in and out of the womb, my God, are you nuts? You will be held accountable for the stand you have taken.

Get out of the party that endorses abortion. Get out of it before you end up in Hell. Repent as never before, beloved. God has a forgiving heart, but after He has asked and waited on you to get your life right with Him, and you don't respond, get ready for all Hell to break loose. Go with God! Go with life! Go with people who trust God. Stay away from evil and evil people.

God hears our cries. I don't like everyone in my party or everyone around me, but I stay clean before the Lord and pray for them.

Forgive everyone. Forgive them rather than opening your mouth and making a fool of yourself. Ask the Lord to help you in this walk of faith.

Years ago, at a Houston Oilers football game (it had to be in the early 1980s), my baby sister and I were getting a hot dog when I noticed a poor lady standing nearby. I was drawn to her and wondered how she got in there. She didn't seem at all interested in football or the stadium atmosphere. She was holding a worn piece of cardboard, and she asked me to sign it. It was a petition to restore prayer back to our schools.

As I looked deeply into that woman's eyes, I came to the realization that she was not a mere woman at all; she was an angel. I was sure of it. Many years have now passed, but I intend to do my part to bring this dream to reality. Will you join me in this effort? You can not only help me restore prayer to our public schools; also help us get the true Christian history about the heritage of our country back into the curriculum.

We need to fire the heads of the Board of Education in each state where these horrible theories are coming from. They started it years ago, and no one stopped them. Now, however, things are different. Let us work together to save our children from this ridiculous critical race theory. Who in the world started this junk? The answer is: Satan himself and all his evil minions who follow him for the love of money and power. Throw them out. We have to do it. If we can restore a godly curriculum, God will bless our endeavors.

This is my vision, my life story, and the assignment the Lord has given to me. Please join me and thousands of other like-minded citizens, and let us win back our country. God made a covenant with our country, the United States of America. Do your own homework. Do your own research, and I'm sure you will reach the same conclusions. I don't know about you, but I'm sick of the evil that has penetrated our cities. Riots! Murders! How bad does it have to get before we, as a nation, start standing up for what is right?

Pray over your family before you venture out into unknown territory. The history of our country is being torn to shreds by evil people all around us. Texas is a good place to live. We Texans believe in the Bible, we believe in God, we believe in right and wrong, and we believe in holding people accountable for their actions. We must now focus on those who are ruining our state and our nation.

What seems to be motivating so much evil is the love of money. The love of money, the Bible says, is the root of all evil. Money itself is not evil. It is the LOVE OF MONEY that is evil. You and I must rise up and change this country. God has given us the right to do this. Don't just hide in your cozy home. I've had four of them, and they never brought me any true happiness! Seeing people saved and filled with the Holy Ghost brings me total joy and peace. It totally changes a person's outlook on life.

Beloved, I can't wait another thirty years to act on what that precious angel encouraged me to do. My sister and I both signed her little cardboard sheet. We signed up do our duty to this country, and I intend to do it. How about you? Will you join us?

Chapter 12

Learning to Forgive As Jesus Forgave

In 2017, I suffered another personal blow when Craig, my husband of twenty-eight years, suddenly passed away. Craig had been a scratch golfer all his life, and he was good at it. Unfortunately, he often suffered from back pain. This led him to the decision to submit to surgery in which a back stimulator would be inserted, and the suggestion of the doctor who recommended it was that this would alleviate his back pain. The idea sounded so good to the both of us that neither of us bothered to do enough research on the dangers of the procedure. Something went wrong during the surgery, and Craig never recovered, dying nine months later as a result of his spinal injuries.

This was devastating for me, and it took me years to forgive the surgeon who had caused my husband's death. But how could I not forgive him? Jesus had forgiven me of so much.

In this sad way, I learned that we must treasure our loved ones as a gift from God and enjoy every minute we have with them. Craig was only seventy when he moved to Heaven. Never take for granted your time on this earth, and love one another as Christ loved the Church.

My heart is heavy for those who do as I did, staying hurt by something someone did to them. I now look back at those who hurt me and pray they are forgiven too. God has a plan for each of us, we are all human, and we all make mistakes. Trusting God is my focus until He calls me home.

Yes, it was a sad day for me when I buried Craig Owen in 2017, and it took me years to finally come out of the resulting grief. Grief is a very strong spirit. I am now taking every

Learning to Forgive As Jesus Forgave

day as a gift from the Lord. He wants us to flourish here on the Earth, and He is getting us ready for the most glorious day of our lives, I do believe—the Rapture of the Church. Are you ready for it?

Bible Portions that Have Blessed Me Through the Years

Daniel 7:10
John 5:17
Numbers 23:23
Isaiah 19:3
Romans 12:1
Philippians 4:6
Ephesians 4 (the entire chapter)
2 Timothy 1:9
Isaiah 1:19
The entire book of Revelation

Another Great Title by Helen Smith Owen

Having the Time of My Life

Helen Smith Owen

Author Contact

You may correspond directly with the author, Helen Smith Owen, at:

warriorwomen77@gmail.com

www.ingramcontent.com/pod-product-compliance
Lightning Source LLC
Chambersburg PA
CBHW031655040426
42453CB00006B/311